CORNISH PRIVIES

by

SHEILA BIRD

COUNTRYSIDE BOOKS

NEWBURY · BERKSHIRE

COUNTRYSIDE BOOKS
3 Catherine Road
Newbury, Berkshire

To view our complete range of books,
please visit us at
www.countrysidebooks.co.uk

ISBN 1 85306 706 7

Photographs by the author unless stated otherwise

Produced through MRM Associates Ltd., Reading
Printed by Woolnough Bookbinding Ltd., Irthlingborough

CONTENTS

FOREWORD

When I began work on this book, I was heartened to discover that so many Cornish privies remain in situ, albeit serving alternative purposes such as storage sheds or duck houses, if not still in use. Whatever their construction or state of repair, each has an individuality and charm of its own, well worth preserving. For apart from being architectural gems, these fascinating little buildings constitute an important part of our social history and heritage. Some are already Listed Buildings.

Initially I approached the project somewhat cautiously, lest folk should perceive it to be a rather delicate subject. But I was soon to discover that the mere mention of privies brought a smile to their faces, and yielded a wonderful wealth of colourful reminiscences. Even the most buttoned-up of my friends and acquaintances waxed lyrical in their enthusiasm to emerge from the closet, fire off wisecracks and get to the crux of the matter.

After carrying out extensive background research into the history of sanitation and studying newspaper and sanitary reports in 19th-century Cornwall, I sought the help of the County Archaeologists, libraries, museums, English Heritage, the National Trust and the local media. I also consulted my 91-year old friend Carrie Ham of Helford Passage, who has the happy knack of tuning others into the everyday domestic scene of her hardworking youth. All this served to provide a springboard for diverse and stimulating explorations around the countryside, visiting archaeological sites, farms, cottages, schools, stately homes, castles and other institutions, enhanced by tea and cake around many a cottage fireside. Some of the most memorable experiences included adventures around the farms, where I first encountered multiple-seater privies, descending to the cells beneath the old Court Room in Bodmin, and meeting some of the steadfast characters who still take the trip down the old garden path in time-honoured style.

The need to answer the most basic call of Nature unites the whole of humanity and the subject provides a remarkable insight into the past, overlooked by the history books. This has been a most worthwhile and enjoyable project, and I am now convinced that we cannot fully identify with the past unless we appreciate the most intimate of daily experiences of those who went before us, whether it be in ancient Rome, the religious houses, royal courts or rural Cornwall. For it was fundamental to life, and reflected and shaped people's attitudes and values. This is as true today as it ever was, and we will not reach sanitary heaven until we learn to be less wasteful with water, and recycle a potential asset, rather than polluting the environment.

I should like to thank the many people who have co-operated so enthusiastically in the creation of the book, making the project such fun.

Sheila Bird

ACKNOWLEDGEMENTS

Bodmin Tourist Information
Bodmin Town Museum
Cornish Guardian
Cornish Studies Library, Redruth
Cornwall Archaeological Unit, Truro
English Heritage
Helston Folk Museum
Lanreath Folk and Farm Museum
National Trust
North Cornwall Gazette
Penryn Museum
Radio Cornwall
Royal Cornwall Museum, Truro
St Ives Museum
The Cornishman
West Briton
Western Morning News

The author thought she was in privy heaven when she discovered her very first two-seater on Luna Farm, on the edge of Bodmin Moor. (Lynn File)

[1]

A POTTED HISTORY

The story of sanitation probably began when the early nomadic tribes created more settled encampments, and turned their attentions to rearing animals and growing crops, rather than hunter-gathering. For communal living inevitably required some organisation in the harnessing of water supplies and the disposal of excrement. The most basic form of sanitation would have been a pit dug in the ground. Some prehistoric latrines, which were likely to have been communal, may have had logs placed across them for comfort and safety, and to have had protective, weatherproof canopies fashioned from branches and readily available vegetation.

Whichever method of dealing with human excrement was employed, our ancient ancestors would have regarded it as a valuable natural resource for enriching the soil, rather than a nuisance to be disposed of. There are a number of Neolithic sites around Cornwall, including the commandingly situated one at Carn Brea, which bears fascinating traces of that period (4000–2500 BC) and of the Iron Age. Visitors to the Romano-Cornish courtyard village of Chysauster, now in the care of English Heritage, can see a clear example of stone-lined drains with capstones and probable stone-lined storage tanks. So water draining from the hillside was taken into the settlement at various points, and released on the lower side. However, the first identifiable Cornish privy dates from medieval times.

The Romans came to Cornwall, attracted, no doubt, by the

Visiting the privy in Roman times was quite a social experience.

mineral wealth lurking beneath the landscape. They seem to have arrived peaceably, rather than flexing military muscles, and to have co-existed with the local population without being too oppressive. There was a Roman fort at Nanstallon, near Bodmin, and a downmarket sort of villa at Magor to the north-west of Camborne, which might be seen as capsules of Roman culture in the Cornish context.

Over the course of many centuries in Britain, there must have been interaction and inter-marriage, with the cultures blending to some extent. Here in Cornwall, the Romans' elaborate plumbing, luxurious bathing and water-flushed latrines, seen in other areas of the country, may have remained low profile. When the Romans were summoned from the outposts of Empire, the void in England was filled by Saxons, Danes, Jutes and other marauders, who destroyed much of the evidence of Roman occupation, and with it the valuable lessons of history on which future generations might build. It held up the progress of plumbing and sanitation, which remained static for about a thousand years.

The communal life of monasteries throughout Europe plays a significant part in the story and the early saints who came to Cornwall from Wales and Ireland established religious foundations close to reliable water supplies. By the 12th century the monks were enjoying some of the benefits of modern plumbing, with hot and cold water supplying kitchens and bathrooms, and latrines which discharged into natural or created streams.

The ablutions areas of some of the finer English religious houses featured the use of stone, lead and marble, and decorative pipework. Some of them had sanitary wings on upper floors, conveniently close to the dormitories. The seats might be arranged in single rows, with partitions and windows, or sometimes back-to-back, with a trench running beneath the sitters. These can be regarded as true privies, in that an effort was made to create privacy for the users. They had to be in a communal context because of the drains, and multi-latrines on account of the religious régime, whereby everyone had to do the same thing at the same time after being summoned by bells. The Abbot usually had his own latrine or necessary house, to spare him the indignity of being seen whilst answering a call of Nature.

In medieval Cornwall, the church was at the influential heart of everyday life. Bodmin possessed a range of religious foundations apart from its fine priory of St Petroc, and there were other priory churches and a profusion of chapels throughout the county. The dramatic and elevated site at St Michael's Mount, which was the focus of pilgrimage, had a 'garderobe' (indoor privy), the exit of which can still be seen on high on the seaward side of the Mount. Thus the weary traveller might gain spectacular relief at journey's end. If Bodmin represents a solid and steadfast religious found-ation, the little chapel of St Michael on Roche Rock, where a hermit took refuge, must rate as the most unlikely and precarious saintly situation. History has omitted to tell us about his sanitary arrangements, but the prudent passer-by would proceed with caution when he gave vent to his most pressing mortal need.

The Roman influence had given rise to the more efficient marketing of tin, in Cornwall, and more extensive farming, and by medieval times farming settlements had expanded right across the county. Some of the medieval longhouses, like those on Bodmin Moor, were set into hillslopes, harnessing reliable water sources and taking advantage of the gradient to aid disposal. The families probably had very down-to-earth outdoor sanitary arrangements, with simple seats set across pits in an outbuilding, with pots or buckets for indoor use. In wintertime they housed their animals beneath the same roof, but at a lower level, and divided from the living quarters by a through passage. They had well organised dairy arrangements, and the effluent from these farming and domestic activities was carried away in carefully constructed drainage channels. The human waste was probably added to the precious resource of the dungheap in the yard.

After the Norman Conquest in 1066, William the Conqueror seized many of the Cornish manors and dispossessed several of the religious houses. In order to hang on to what they had gained, the Normans built some formidable castles to deter their enemies, and more castles were constructed over the next few centuries. Some of the striking stone castles that we see today, such as Launceston, Tintagel, Trematon and Restormel, would have had garderobes. These were usually built into the ample thickness of the walls, above vertical shafts. They could be situated unobtrusively within a buttress, or corbelled out in a projecting turret with an open drop or exit rather than a shaft, to create an architectural feature. Garderobes on several floors might be served by multiple shafts resembling chimney flues, discharging down the face of outer walls, into cesspits or removable barrels. Those built into chimney breasts tended to be a little warmer. The historic garderobes that we see today seem very stark, but there would have been spacious wooden seats, floor coverings and various personal touches to make conditions as comfortable as possible for the sitters. The garderobe exits did not usually incorporate any means of flushing, although rainwater was sometimes harnessed in the hope of sweetening things up a bit. It could be argued that garderobe exits weakened the defences, allowing agile enemy entry. But by the same token it offered a more subtle deterrent, in the form of deep, stinking moats and slippery walls covered in excrement.

At Restormel we have the certain remains of late 13th-century garderobes and a possible out-flow to another in the castle keep. The courtyard buildings are arranged in circular fashion, and there is a garderobe built into the thickness of the wall on ground level. Another is built into the wall near the kitchens, on what would have been the first floor. Tangible evidence of garderobes exists too in the castle keep at Launceston, which was probably the most important town in Cornwall in medieval times. This castle, built on the site of an earlier one, was known as 'Castle Terrible'. George Fox, the famous Quaker who was incarcerated here on account of his religious beliefs, found the sanitation less than desirable, referring to its 'most filthy dungeon, called Doomsdale'. Archaeologists have also found evidence of domestic areas and latrines in the ruined priory of St Thomas, founded in 1127 by the Augustinians.

By the 14th century Cornwall had a network of towns and markets which attracted people from all over the countryside, but one can only speculate about the facilities for visitors which may or may not have existed. The ancient port of Lostwithiel had strong links with the Dukes of Cornwall and a fine administrative Duchy Palace was built here. Royalty no doubt had their own personalised arrangements if they decided to pay a call – this would have taken the form of a garderobe or close-stool – but dungheaps, stinks and squalor lurked around some of the hovels and alleyways of the town itself. Taprell House, now in use as a library, has on its first floor a garderobe dating from the late 16th century. The historic old town must have trembled at the time of the Civil War, when about 15,000 Parliamentarian soldiers were quartered here, taking over

Restormel Castle and the most prestigious buildings. They created havoc, and the sanitary situation must have been diabolical.

St Mawes and Pendennis castles, built by Henry VIII to protect the Fal estuary from French attack and now in the care of English Heritage, offer good opportunities to relate to those times and the concept of garderobes. At Pendennis a garderobe in the Governor's Lodge has a discreetly disguised door which merges with the panelled walls. There is also a small window in the granite lobby, and recesses in the walls which once supported a wooden seat. The opening falls away to an area known as the Cavaliers' Kitchen. As there were no dungeons as such, and this was where the Napoleonic prisoners might have been held, there is some speculation about them experiencing the fetid effects of the fall-out. There is another latrine set into the thickness of the wall of the kitchen, where odours must have merged with the appetising smell of the cooking. It is thought that Charles II, who stayed at Pendennis on his escape to the Isles of Scilly, may well have used the governor's garderobe.

One might imagine royalty to have been at the cutting edge of civilised sanitation, but the religious houses were leading the way in matters of hygiene and cleanliness, until Henry VIII dissolved the monasteries. For centuries royalty retained a rather self indulgent attachment to their personalised close-stools, chamber pots and piss-pots, which had to be emptied by their servants. At the end of the 16th century, Sir John Harington, the handsome, dashing, witty, scholarly godson of Elizabeth I, who was sickened by the sanitary squalor of his time, studied the lessons of history, and invented a flushing water-closet with working parts. This consisted of a pan and seat with a cistern above, an overflow pipe, a valve and a waste with a water seal. He installed one in

Garderobe in the Governor's Lodge, Pendennis Castle, Falmouth. (Photo courtesy of English Heritage)

his house near Bath, and made one for the Queen at Richmond Palace. She thanked him very much, and carried on using her close-stool.

The sanitary arrangements for ordinary people in Cornwall and the rest of Britain remained static and very basic until the late 19th century, and often beyond that. Many cottagers took to the fields, woods or foreshore to answer the call of Nature. Some kept receptacles for the 'night-soil' in their homes, which were emptied on fields, gardens or gutters in the street, while more fortunate folk had earth closets set in detached buildings known as privies at the far end of the garden, as far away from dwelling houses as possible. But the problems of waste disposal became more acute as people gravitated towards larger centres of population like London, where accumulations of filth created health hazards. Some of the wealthier townsfolk had latrines emptying into cesspits in their gardens, cellars or even beneath living room floorboards, which had to be cleared out periodically. In medieval times well paid 'gongfermors' went round with carts. In later times these treasures of society came to be known as nightmen, although they sometimes perambulated around during the day, and were sometimes women. In the days before Political Correctness, one of the nightmen went around crying, 'Women! Women! Bring out your dungses!'

A cheaper, more popular method of ridding households of the contents of smelly slop buckets was to off-load them into street gutters. In some places the more considerate folk might cry the traditional warning of 'Gardy Loo!' (Watch out! Water!) before flinging the odious contents of the privy pots from upper windows. (I can well relate to the hazards of passers by, for as a small child I narrowly escaped the flying contents of a receptacle being emptied from the upper balcony of the almshouses in Tregony, as I whizzed down the hill on my bike. And I'm sure it had a handle!)

Some progress had been made towards a cleaner life during the 17th century, as the result of pestilence. Although the streets were still filthy, efforts were made towards organised sanitation and the creation of water supplies, paving the way for the development of water closets. By the 18th century public sewers were being constructed, and rather basic water closets were making their appearance in houses and gardens. However, it was not all sweetness and light, for the indoor ones tended to be placed in some convenient corner without windows or ventilation, and the effluent taken through an unventilated system to the sewer or cesspit. Lead, marble and later pottery were used in the manufacture of water closets. Around 1710 Queen Anne was provided with a little 'place of easement' at Windsor Castle, where there was a marble water closet with wash-down sluices.

People were becoming more aware of the desirability of keeping clean, and some were fortunate enough to enjoy the luxury of having baths in their own homes. Baths with ornate bath houses, like the one at Antony, near Torpoint in Cornwall, also became fashionable in the late 18th century. However, water closets and household baths were the prerogative of the few, and ordinary folk fetched water from the springs and wells and bathed in small metal tubs by cottage firesides. As far as 18th-century England was concerned, they were just beginning to catch up with the Minoans of 1400 BC, in regard to wholesome sanitation.

Inspired by Rome: the 18th-century Bath House at Antony, near Torpoint, with the Bath House Pool to the left. This elegant building housed a seawater plunge bath and a panelled changing room. It was open to the sky, and partially roofed over in the style of a Roman atrium. (Photo courtesy of the National Trust)

No particular individual can be credited with having invented the water closet, as successive sanitary engineers built on the discoveries of those who had gone before, improving the designs and discarding the faults. Scottish born Alexander Cummings, an accomplished clock and watchmaker, took out the first British patent for a water closet. It had a pan with a sliding valve across the bottom. Thomas Prosser improved on this a couple of years later, and in 1778 Joseph Bramah made further refinements, including a hinged valve under the pan, instead of a sliding valve. Pulling a handle opened the valve and released the excrement, and pushing it down again closed the valve and activated a delaying mechanism which ensured that the pan

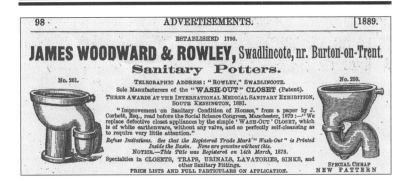

was sweet and wholesome for the next person. Although there was some water seepage, and the complexity of the design predisposed it to occasional hiccups, Bramah's beautifully made water closets sold well and stood the test of time. The quality of his workmanship was such that his name came to be incorporated in the language, in that the colloquial expression 'bramah', signified anything of top quality.

During the 19th century the designing of sanitary ware became quite a challenge, and elegant bathroom furnishings and a variety of water closets, including portable closets with cisterns, appeared on the scene. The enterprising sanitary engineers faced a challenge in promoting their wares in a culture where things lavatorial were never mentioned in polite society. Daniel Thomas Bostel, of Bostel Brothers of Brighton, caused Victorian ladies to blush when he exhibited his Excelsior wash-out closet in 1875. The situation became a little more relaxed when the Twyfords, descendants of Joshua Twyford the Staffordshire potter, came on the scene, in an alliance of art and engineering. The Twyfords produced a wash-out closet called the 'National' in 1881, with its works concealed beneath a wooden framework. This proved very popular, and they followed it up a couple of years later with the highly efficient and very beautiful 'Unitas', which achieved worldwide success. They knew how to advertise in the right quarters, and their exquisite catalogues helped the word 'Unitas' to become synonymous with excellence. Doultons, founded in 1851, also produced very beautiful catalogues, and enjoyed some distinguished patronage; they received the Royal Warrant in 1901. Other stirring names used by the great designers included the 'Deluge', 'Torrent', 'Axis', 'Orion' and 'Cardinal' and these caught the imagination of the public.

If the wonderful achievements of the 19th-century sanitary engineers had enabled excrement to be flushed out of sight and out of mind – like magic, it was not a case of sanitary heaven. The coming of the water closet may have solved a lot of problems, but it threw up a formidable range of new ones. The water closet spared folk the inconvenience of taking the trip down the old garden path in all types of weather, and the sickening job of emptying the privy bucket, but invisible and inescapable dangers might have been lurking beneath their roofs. These included the hazards of sewer gases inside their homes, as a result of incompetent plumbing, and bacteria-laden water where the contents of drains had leached into the pipework of the mains supplies. Waterborne pollution of the environment, spread over a wider area was an ever-present hazard, and disease was rife.

A scholary and idealistic vicar, the Revd Henry Moule of Fordington in Dorset, appalled by a cholera epidemic in his parish in the 1850s, gave a lot of thought to the matter. He considered the privy vault and cesspool to be unnatural abominations, and blamed the water closet for making an unhealthy situation much worse. Water merely carried off

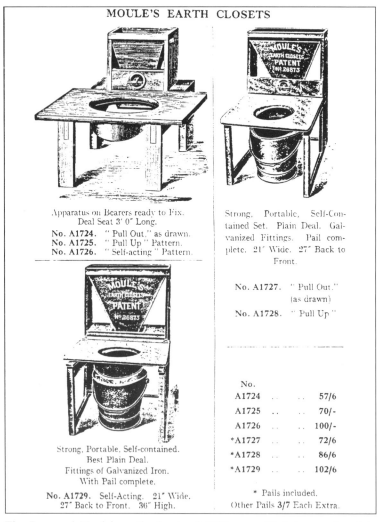

MOULE'S EARTH CLOSETS

Apparatus on Bearers ready to Fix.
Deal Seat 3' 0" Long.
No. A1724. " Pull Out," as drawn.
No. A1725. " Pull Up " Pattern.
No. A1726. " Self-acting " Pattern.

Strong, Portable, Self-Contained Set. Plain Deal. Galvanized Fittings. Pail complete. 21" Wide. 27" Back to Front.

No. A1727. " Pull Out."
(as drawn)
No. A1728. " Pull Up "

Strong, Portable, Self-contained.
Best Plain Deal.
Fittings of Galvanized Iron.
With Pail complete.
No. A1729. Self-Acting. 21" Wide.
27" Back to Front. 36" High.

No.		
A1724	..	57/6
A1725	..	70/-
A1726	..	100/-
*A1727	..	72/6
*A1728	..	86/6
*A1729	..	102/6

* Pails included.
Other Pails 3/7 Each Extra.

The Reverend Moule's earth closets of 1860 were still being produced in the 1930s.

offensive matter without effectively absorbing and deodorising it. Practising what he preached, he filled in his cesspool and instructed his large family to use buckets instead. This led to the discovery that dry earth sprinkled on the contents of the privy bucket absorbed it efficiently and dispelled unpleasant odours. Furthermore, experiments with this natural fertiliser on the soil produced good results. He took out patents on the Moule Earth Closets in 1860, 1869, and 1873, and his company produced a range of models incorporating some ingenious devices, at prices to suit everyone. In its simplest form there would be a wooden seat over a bucket, where the pulling of a handle would release a covering of fine dry earth from a hopper set at a higher level, to the rear. Sometimes the release was activated by the user rising from the seat. Ironmongers were still selling 'moules' at least until 1940 and some were still in use 100 years after the first patent.

SPOTLIGHT ON 19TH-CENTURY CORNWALL

The *West Briton* of 9th March 1827 reported the words of Clement Carlyon MD who had been studying the causes of typhus in Cornwall and its *Connection with want of Cleanliness about the Habitations chiefly of the Lower Classes of Society*: 'Nothing has a greater tendency to debase the lower orders of the community than dirty habitations and slovenly habits. And at the present day, when cottages and small tenements are springing up like mushrooms, in every direction, it is more than ever to be regretted that, in their construction and arrangement, so little attention is paid to the essential points of cleanliness and health . . . A traveller through the mining districts of Cornwall, will perceive that most of the cottages spread out around him, have been built under very great disadvantages of soil and situation . . . spruce gardens, surrounded with a low wall in front, and the green meadows adjoining, impart an air of cleanliness and neatness, which naturally lead to the persuasion that such must be the abodes of well regulated families. Yet even of these, the courtlets will be too frequently found deficient in commodious and cleanly arrangement.

'In parts of the County not connected with mines, we shall find the same, or a greater neglect of cleanliness. The wretched cob-built cottages, scattered over the country, have, almost invariably, open catch-pits close to them, and I scarcely know a single village or church-town, where the same nuisance may not be seen before the very doors and windows of the houses. Nor is the evil by any means confined to the country – our towns are sadly negligent of measures conducive to the health of the inhabitants: and the lower classes, in particular might almost always be better accommodated than they are, with mutal benefit to themselves and their landlords. . .'

It is rather surprising that the builders of new houses in the early 19th century placed so little importance on the need for sanitary arrangements, when they had the means to indulge themselves in creating neat and pretty gardens. People living in the older cob-built cottages with earthen-ware floors, a single multi-purpose room downstairs and one or two small bedrooms above, often had large families and lived in squalor. In the absence of any sanitary facilities inside or outside, they used chamber pots and slop buckets, which they emptied on dungheaps just outside the door, or resorted to the fields and woods in the time-honoured way. The writer of this report thought that Sticker, near St Austell was a village typifying catchpits of the sort which were 'the bane of Cornish cottages' lives'. In a bid to encourage them to improve their habits, the Breage Cottage Gardening Society, founded in 1834, offered prizes for 'the Cottages which are best covered with Roses or other Creepers, providing the dung-pit be not in front of the door'.

If things were bad in the countryside, these evils were greatly intensified in the backs streets of the Cornish towns, where lack of space and light led to putrid piles of manure from their pigs, night-soil and offal. Strangely, few folk seem to have made the connection between filth and disease, and even when it was pointed out, they were reluctant to change their ways. The official investigations carried out at that time provide a rare insight into the 19th-century sanitary scene in Cornwall, where some walked down the old garden path to the earth closet in the privy, some had indoor or outdoor water closets, and a surprising number had no facilities at all. In fact, there would have been some who relied on slop pails or took to the great outdoors in virtually every town and village in the county. Where privies existed at the beginning of the 19th century, they would have taken the form of earth closets, situated in little buildings as far removed from the dwelling houses as possible. They were often screened by shrubs and flowers and sweet smelling vegetation, and seldom had any windows.

Earth closets might be set in stone-built outhouses, as often happened on farms, where they might be multi-seaters, in galvanised iron sheds, or wooden structures of the sentry box type. There was sometimes a reluctance to take responsibility for the repair and maintenance of these privies, particularly when the facilities were shared by several families. There was an occasional Nimby tendency to nip out and dump the offensive contents of the privy on someone else's patch at dead of night, but this was usually in the more built-up areas, for country folk used it on their gardens, and grew remarkably fine rhubarb. Unless the privies were kept in good repair, they soon became dilapidated and began to rot. When times were really hard, householders might chop up the door of the privy or knock out some of the planking for firewood. Sometimes they were used as chicken houses, leaving the families privy-less. In the central part of Copperhouse, near Hayle, a sanitary inspector found a sentry box privy used by two families to be leaning over backwards at such an angle that it threatened to take some unfortunate user to Eternity. At Angarrack he saw a row of five wooden privies in a very filthy and ruinous condition, capable of bringing disease and death. The floors were rotten and crumbling, and the roofs in the process of collapsing. The excrement had filled the shallow trenches underneath, and built up until it appeared above the seats of some of the privies.

The most basic of earth closets consisted of wooden seats set above holes in the ground, where earth or ashes were used to cover the excrement. This would be removed from an opening at the rear of the building, and used as a fertiliser on fields and gardens. If the effluent was not used in this way, it tended to end up in some odious catch-pit or causing pollution elsewhere. In June 1839, Francis Lean of Twelveheads fell foul of the law by depositing the contents of his privy in St Clement Street, Truro, during the daytime. This was a particularly bad time of year to do such a thing, creating unpleasantness for passers-by, and was contrary to the statute permitting such operations to be carried out between the hours of 11 pm, and 4 am. Few people in Camborne had any means of sanitation, and those who did were found to have particularly foul 'petties'. In 1852 the *West Briton* reported that the putrid contents of these privies

24

Space was tight for the creation of privies in many Cornish towns. Disposal was a problem, and men were employed to go around with their 'honey carts', collecting the 'night-soil'. Some of the privies pictured here now contain water closets, which are still in use.

were carried through the streets during the daytime, 'in defiance of the common rules of prudence and decency, a practice, in which, in most towns would be punished by a penalty.'

The desire to harness the potential of tourism eventually caused some places to look to their laurels and by the 1880s most of the Cornish towns and some of the villages had mains water supplies and the use of wash-out, wash-down or flush water closets.

The village of Kilkhampton, in the far north of the county, was partly sewered and partly drained by waste water gutters running in front of the houses. These households used earth privies or pail closets, situated as far from the dwellings as possible. Kilkhampton seems to have come out smelling of roses, for, all in all, the sanitary inspector regarded the place as being 'better than the average of Cornish villages'. As the authorities focused their attentions on places with serious problems, it would seem that the rural areas of northern Cornwall enjoyed a better track record than most other parts of the county. This was probably because of their remoteness, and their continued use of the old-fashioned earth closets, whereby they recycled their own effluent and grew fine vegetables.

At Penzance, St Ives and other coastal points, however, it was a long standing custom for the men to go down to the foreshore to relieve themselves. Ladies Rock, at St Ives, recalls the days when their wives also honoured the same tradition. This habit led to the establishment of five strategically-placed public latrines for men, in the fishing

The 'Iron Duke' urinal outside the old railway station at Wadebridge, which have both been swept away. (Photo courtesy of the Royal Cornwall Museum, Truro)

Museum curator Brian Stephens takes the author on a conducted tour of the privies of St Ives.

quarter, where household closets were virtually non-existent. Automatic flushes discharged every twenty minutes, and a man was employed to take care of these latrines. At Newlyn and Mousehole, where there were few privies or water closets and fisherman fouled the foreshore in the time-honoured way, it was officially proposed that some automatically flushed trough closets, of the type they used when visiting the port of St Ives, be established in convenient spots.

The old fishing town of St Ives was becoming a resort by the late 19th century. Although well-heeled visitors may have regarded clusters of tiny cottages amongst courts and alleyways climbing up the hillsides as charming and picturesque, the confined situation made it difficult for the inhabitants to find enough space to create proper closet accommodation. Those who had no water closets used pail

27

or midden privies. The pails, used by the women and children, had their contents covered over with ashes and remained indoors in the bedroom chimney or behind a screen, before the tide was right for the daily emptying on the foreshore. Despite all the problems, their houses were kept neat and tidy, and the sturdy folk of St Ives escaped the serious cholera epidemics.

To sum up this quick gallop through privy history, the 19th century had seen an increase in piped water supplies and sewage schemes in some developing towns throughout the country, where water closets appeared in outhouses or in convenient corners of people's homes. Meanwhile, those in

The Armitage Shanks unit in the sluice room at Lanhydrock (National Trust), where the housemaids would have emptied the bed pans and slop buckets. The slops were put down the pan on the right hand side, then flushed away into the main sewer, and the receptacles were washed in the sink on the left.

The pleasing architecture of a pair of traditional privies, serving farmworkers' cottages in the parish of St Martin-in-Meneage.

A privy and wash-house at Portreath.

rural areas continued to fetch water from the wells and springs, and take the traditional journey down the garden path – if they were fortunate enough to have one. In the 20th century, there was an increased awareness of the desirability of proper piped water and sewage systems, heightened during the Second World War by the arrival of the Americans, who thought our rustic ways were quaint and demanded more civilised standards.

At the beginning of the 20th century, many people were enjoying the luxury of indoor sanitation, baths, hot and cold running water, with hi-tech developments taking the drudgery out of washday and other household chores. Although towns and some villages were enjoying mod cons by the mid-20th century, many country folk were still fetching water from springs or standpipes, and trotting down the garden path when Nature called.

[2]

'E DONE THE JOB

Before being invited to produce this book, the world of privies, Jeyes Fluid, newspaper (in lieu of toilet paper), rhubarb, slop pails and chamber pots was unchartered territory. So prior to embarking on my voyage of discovery I decided to get to the bottom of the matter, by consulting my old friend, 91-year-old Carrie Ham of Helford Passage, who had been a farmer's wife, and who knew about these things.

'It's very polite for you to call 'em privies,' she said, in response to my first, tentative enquiry. 'We use t'er call 'em something different from that. . . Ho! ho! ho!' 'What did you call them? Go on, tell me. We want to capture the essence of how things really were.' 'Shit 'ouses! That's what we use t'er call 'em! Well, that's what the men called 'em, anyway.' 'What did the ladies call them?' 'The ladies use ter call 'em toilets,' she declared, taking on a ladylike sort of pose. 'We are talking about the 1930s. We were farming; we rented the farm just after we were married. We were really, really off the road, and our toilet was up the end of the garden, in a little shed. And inside this shed was a wooden seat. Well, this poor ole seat would just lift off, and there was a bucket affair underneath. And for toilet paper we use ter cut out squares of newspaper, and thread 'em through and 'ang 'em up on a nail. The children use ter make these. It was their job. . . Cut up newspapers into about six inch squares, an' then they'd thread 'em through. 'Ave a big darning needle or something, an' thread 'em through, an' tie a knot. There was a little nail they use ter 'ang 'em on. And people used all that

31

for toilet paper. 'Twent on for years an' years. We 'ad no toilet paper. We was always afraid t' use it, because it's such a modern luxury.

'Down the end of the garden there was a pit. We use ter keep one end of the garden special for the lavatory buckets. When the bucket was filled, we'd take it down and put it in the pit, and dig another pit by the side and use the earth to cover it over. So the new pit was ready for the next load. You'd do it in rotation in the spare bit o' ground. So that's what we did all the time we were there. Ours was quite modern, compared with the next farm. They'd got two 'oles in their seat; one for grown ups and one for children. 'Twas in a little wooden shed with no back, an' all open to the elements. . .' 'So they would've got really cold and wet?' 'Oh, yes, you'd 'ave ter put up with that! They 'ad like a sentry box, with two sides and a door at the front. People would go in and shut the door and everything, but there was no back to it; no back at all. There was also no bucket, and nothing to catch anything. So everything went straight on the ground. Whenever they wanted to clean it out, they'd go to the back of this open shed with a bucket and wheelbarrow, and cart it away to somewhere on the farm, and then they'd start all over again. But mostly the lavatories were used by the women and children. The men use ter go out beside the hedges, where they were working. They didn't bother. 'Twas only more to empty.'

'What about nocturnal visits to the privy?' I asked. 'Night-time, you 'ad ter get up as best you could. You'd light up the old oil lantern, make your way up the garden path and put it down on the floor of the toilet. There would be nowhere to 'ang it. 'Twas all very private, 'cos 'twas only you that lived on the farm.' She paused, and looked nostalgic. 'The shit 'ouse . . . 'Twas all very well made; 'twas 'omemade, mostly.

But they lasted years an' years an' years. We didn't think nothin' of it, for 'twas all like that in the olden days in the country.

'There is a story, well 'tis only a story that I 'eard, but I thought 'twas very good, 'bout a little house up in the corner. There was a soldier came 'ome on leave, an' 'e was tellin' 'is father 'ow 'and grenades worked. An' 'e said,' "Now I'll show you Dad, 'ow it works. I'll throw one up the garden an' you shall see 'ow it goes off." So 'e threw it, and BANG! It went off just outside the privy. "Oh, my gosh!" said Father. "Mother's in there!" An' they rushed up. "Mother! Mother! Are you all right?" "Oh," said Mother, "I think it must've been something I ate!"'

Having been initated into the early 20th-century sanitary scene so graphically, and so delightfully, I felt ready to embark on my adventures around the county, in pursuit of the quintessential part of our domestic heritage. So I decided to make contact with the Lanreath Folk and Farm Museum, run by the Facey family, who made me very welcome. Birdsong filled the air on that sunny September morning, as Leila Facey led me into the back garden to see their handsome privy in its leafy setting. It was the very first privy I had ever photographed, and I thought it was a little architectural gem. 'Three generations of my husband's family have lived here, and at least two generations had to use the privy, because there was no mains water or sewerage in the village until 1952. At the moment it is being used for storing things. It's a handy place to keep coal and logs, because we still have an open fire in the farmhouse sitting room. When it was a working privy I think it just had a wooden seat with two holes in. Underneath, it was as though

Leila Facey outside the handsome mellowed privy on the family farm at Lanreath, which has assumed a certain whimsical charm.

there was a box, with one side missing, and everything sort of slid out onto the field behind. They were called earth closets in the main, weren't they? I think there was a certain amount of earth to cover everything, and it got pushed out through the gap, with a slight incline. Then people used it on their gardens. It was a very primitive arrangement. I didn't come here until 1953, and fortunately we didn't have to go out into the garden to use the toilet then.

'There were one or two cottages in the village that had no second door. There was only the one door, and there was no water or sanitation inside. And I used to wonder quite often how they managed or where they got rid of their effluent. . .' This touched a chord with my 19th-century background research. 'Out in the fields and woods, or by stealth at night, on someone else's patch,' I ventured.

Leila escorted me down the road to the museum, where there was a fascinating array of farm implements, and rural and domestic artefacts, including a downmarket commode and a traditional white enamel slop bucket with a lid. Her sister-in-law, Marion Facey, who used to run the museum, and who was hanging out the washing next door commented: 'I can remember my grandmother having a commode like that. She always kept it beside the bed, because the toilet was outside the house. You had to go downstairs, out the back door, around the side path to an old stone shed with a corrugated roof. It was covered in brambles and stinging nettles and spiders, and things like that. I can appreciate having modern conveniences today, because I can remember using my grandmother's loo, where you had to go outside at dead of night. It was never a very pleasant experience having to go to the loo, you know. This was down near St Austell, in the china clay district. The mains came in with the next owner, in 1960.'

35

I was soon to discover that one thing led to another, in the course of researching this book, and back in the farmhouse kitchen, Leila's daughter Kathryn Strang told me about the 2-seater privy at Luna Farm on the edge of Bodmin Moor, where she had gone as a young bride. She used to joke about her primitive privy, although she had a modern toilet just outside the door, at the end of the pighouses. Her grandmother would admonish her for such frivolity, pointing out that this was the reality of life for her, in her young days. Luna Farm had been sold, and a quick phone call from Kathryn put me on track for my next few adventures.

At Luna Farm I was greeted warmly by Lynn File, who felt very privileged to have a 2-seater privy in her garden. I felt elated to have experienced my first sighting of a 2-seater so early in my explorations. I had arrived; I was in sanitary heaven!

Margery Worden, now living in Lostwithiel, told me that she and her sister spent four years with their grandparents at Luna in the early 1930s, when their father was confined to hospital, and their mother was training to be a nurse. 'There was a courtyard at the back at that time. There were pig houses along there, a privy and a pumphouse, and everything was cleaned out into the yard, including the privy. It was a 2-seater; one for small people.' Opinion seems to be divided on whether people used these multiple seaters at the same time, and those who have never been associated with them tend to feel uncomfortable about the idea. Margery thought that small children would have done, for safety's sake. 'That big hole was rather large, and they'd have fallen down in it, or something like that,' she said, and recalled that it was no fun going out there on a dark winter's night, in the wind and the rain. 'You took a lantern in those days, you know. A candle wouldn't have been any good in that exposed situation, because it would have blown out. Torches weren't about in those days. It was paraffin lanterns, with a wire and spring. You'd pull them up, and you'd light the wick.'

Margery's sister, Mary Littleton, now of St Austell, recalled the elder tree which was planted near the privy at Luna, for it was a widespread country belief that these trees kept the flies away. They certainly created more privacy, enhanced the beauty of the setting, and sweetened the air with the fragrance of their flowers. 'When they cleaned out the privy, they used to scrape it all up, put it on the dungheap, then spread it all over the fields. Everything was recycled in those days. It was more environmentally friendly. They used to recycle everything, and use their wits.' Those were the days of rook pie, workmen toiling in the fields and rewards of home-made cider, ham and junket and roast beef in the middle of the day. If this privy could speak, what a story it could tell of fringe-of-moorland farming in days of yore.

Margery remembered another privy with two seats at Hilltown Farm, near St Neot. 'Instead of two seats on the same level, they had one at a slightly lower level; not too high off the ground.' 'The small ones could sit on it with their feet on the ground,' agreed Mary. 'I know my uncle used to cut up the *Radio Times* into little sheets, and put them on a piece of binder twine and hang them up in there. There wasn't toilet paper before the war. Our great aunt, who was an elderly lady in her eighties, lived in half a house at St Neot. She had to walk quite a long way to her lavatory, which was down through a shrubbery and down the garden by the river. But she kept a bucket upstairs, which she would empty once a day. If you were caught short out in the country, you used a dock leaf, didn't you? If you were on your way to school and you got caught short, you went behind a hedge and used a dock leaf.' As far as one senior relative was concerned, her problems were quite the reverse, when she left Luna for a few days. For on her return she announced, 'Well, I didn't manure their land!' Hopefully she restored the *status quo*, on being re-united with the privy.

The Arthur family from nearby Lestow have a lovely old, ivy-capped privy at the edge of the farmyard that has survived a number of changes which have taken place over the last century. As Lewis and his son Colin explained to me, the original farmhouse was pulled down about a hundred years ago, and the privy was associated with that. The present farmhouse always had indoor sanitation. This privy would formerly have stood at the bottom of the large garden, where a big shed has been erected in recent times. 'So they literally walked down the old garden path to the privy,' declared Colin, demonstrating an appreciation of privy culture. 'We thought we was goin' t' 'ave t' take it down when we built the

This much cherished privy beneath a mantle of ivy at Lestow Farm now houses a water closet, and remains viable.

the shed, but we managed t' get away with it,' said his father. 'As it wasn't necessary to knock it down, we decided to leave it as a sort of memento to the old house,' added Colin.

We admired the well constructed privy from all angles but the heavy mantle of vegetation obscured the details of the roof construction. 'Well, that was a slate "peggy" roof,' explained Lewis. 'Well, "peggies" we call 'en. The reason is the slates are held in with wood pegs. 'Tis only our name for it'.

Today the privy may almost have disappeared from view beneath its outsize canopy of foliage, but it remains functional as a water closet; convenient for the family, and intriguing for their guests, particularly at party time. When it comes to small talk and lavatorial humour, it provides their visitors with something to go on.

While I was on the Moor, I decided to look up my friend Arthur Richards, who had worked on farms throughout the area all his life. He lives in a remote cottage a mile off the road, near Minions, without mod cons, and is a happy and contented man who walks with the aid of two sticks. His charming cottage in its idyllic setting was originally one of three and occupies a site of great antiquity. To my surprise and delight he escorted me around his wooded back garden, and showed me no less than three privies. One was ancient, stone-built and had virtually disappeared beneath the undergrowth; one was old, with a ruined, galvanised charm all of its own, and the other was a contemporary inter-pretation on a traditional theme. His parents moved here in 1948 with their five children, and at that time Mrs Sanders was living next door with her five daughters, with one privy serving both dwellings. 'Mother said 't wouldn't be right for us to use the same lavatory that six women was using. So we saw the landlord, an' 'e said use the galvanised one down the garden, which was originally used by the ruined house on

Arthur Richards decided that it was time to think about a new privy when the widening gaps in the corroding walls provided a bit too much ventilation.

the other side, which used t' be a pub. Well, the old galvanised one got rusted through, an' the roof started leakin'. So I 'ad a more modern one. Only been there p'raps ten years. It came down the lane in sections, an' my brother put 'en t'gether, like. Inside, I 'ad to 'ave something like a chair, with arms, t' let m'self down, like. 'E cut the bottom out of the chair, an' put the Elsan bucket in there.' He thought that this ingenious, personalised arrangement suited him very well.

Publicity in regard to my researching the Cornish privy, spaced out over several months, had started to yield a wealth of fascinating material, including an invitation from Chris and Dave Braddon at Fiddlers Green, near St Newlyn East, to visit the brick-built privy (now a potting shed) at the bottom of the garden of their 200-year-old miner's cottage. I was to find that many of the privies in this area were constructed of brick, but not all of them had enjoyed the TLC that the Braddons had bestowed on this one. 'The privy has been re-roofed, using some of the existing slate, and the existing ridge. The door itself; that came from the old school at Tresillian,' explained Dave, who carried out the work himself. 'I've got a builder friend who did some work over there, and he offered me a load of firewood, amongst which were the old doors from Tresillian School. As you can see, they were painted red. So we kept them red, to keep them as original as possible, although you can see there's new hinges gone on.' The preservation of privies, and realignment of their purpose, was to be an interesting, recurring theme.

Nearby farmer Steve Collins suggested that I should have a look at the old privies on his property. The first we reached was a late-1950s-style one, built by his grandfather and

Steve Collins by the 1950s-style concrete privy, just outside the back door of the farmhouse, and adjacent to the well which still supplies water for all farm and domestic purposes.

housing a water closet. It was constructed of concrete, and it was remarkable in that the roof consisted of a single concrete slab. Once despised, concrete and corrugated iron have recently come into focus in their own right, as playing a part in our architectural heritage. Furthermore, it was constructed as a water closet, harnessing the waters of the adjacent 30-foot well, which supplies the whole farm and an area beyond, with a highly ingenious pump and gravity system. 'The whole farm feeds off gravity,' explained Steve. 'All the water for the sheep and cattle, for the drains, for the outside toilet. . . Everything you want.' They levered up the well cover, and I was fascinated by the ingenuity of past generations, and of the craftsmanship of the stonework. A separate system pumps the water into the kitchen for drinking purposes and a man from Carrick Council comes around to take samples every so often. I was to discover that quite a few places, especially farms, have their own independent water supply today.

If this was a comparatively modern privy, we were just about to discover one which was rooted in antiquity. 'That's a proper bucket job,' he explained. 'Father would dig holes in the garden, and I didn't know what the holes were for. I had a friend the other side of the village, whose dad used to do the same. When he was asked why there was a hole in the garden his dad would say, "Oh, the tortoise is out; we dug a 'ole t' trap 'en."' Father appeared at the back door. 'We're just going up to the cottage. Going to 'ave a look at the outside toilet, if we can get anywhere near it,' said Steve. 'You used t' dig the pits over there to empty it, didn't you, Father?' Father looked a little sheepish, then chuckled. 'Well, it's a bit embarrassin', talkin' about those days, isn't it? With all the mod cons they got now!' Then, warming to the theme, he added, 'Well, that was always a job, that was, wasn't it? That was done in the dark, that was.' His eyes lit up at the recollection. 'Yeah, that was the bucket an' chuck it! Put 'en in the garden.'

By the time we reached the old privy, a good natured band of helpers had appeared and were hacking a way through the brambles and undergrowth, to create a path to the little ivy-clad building at the bottom of the garden. These are the sort of adventures that writers relish – all in the name of duty. As I made my way through the parted undergrowth, I half expected to see a Sleeping Beauty or, better still, a handsome prince appearing on a white charger, but a voice saying it was constructed of stone blocks with an asbestos slate roof, brought me back to this dreamlike reality. 'Tongue an' groove door; proper wood. That's good hard wood,' Steve declared. 'It's never been changed in all the years.' The door opened inwards, and there was a latch, but no bolt. Privies very rarely had bolts or locks; that was all part of the culture. The wooden seat was shaped to fit the bucket beneath it, with a wooden lid to seal it off when it was not in use, and it was set on a substantially built solid concrete floor.

I later pondered on the reasons for 2-seaters and inward opening doors with John and David Hopkins at Trewinnion Farm, Summercourt. 'I have visions of two people sharing a newspaper when they're sitting on the toilet,' said David. In spite of the difficulties of manoeuvring round it we decided that an inward opening door would be in the interests of safety and weather resistance. 'And you can put yer foot against it!' laughed his father, John, speaking from experience.

THE MORE THE MERRIER

Derek and Anne Thomas took occupation of Colan Barton, near St Columb, in 1969, not realising until they got there

The old privy at Colan Barton with its two big holes and a smaller one as if for Father Bear, Mother Bear and Baby Bear. (Photograph by Anna Machin Weaver)

that the only convenience was a 3-holer out in the garden. Derek said there were two big holes and a smaller one. It had the traditional pointed door and no windows, and was emptied from the back. They settled in and made use of the privy for several months – until the occasion that Derek had to make a swift and sudden emergency call in the middle of the night. 'Can you imagine getting out of bed on a very cold night . . . to go down the stairs, out the front door, down the garden path – to an outside loo that didn't have any flushing facilities, had no light, and was draughty? No! That was it! We had indoor facilities put in right away!'

Judith Bryant of Sworne Farm, in the parish of St Martin-in-Meneage, recalled a 3-seater privy at her childhood home in Mullion, which has sadly been destroyed after becoming dilapidated and overgrown with ivy. Her mother attributed the tradition of multiple-seaters to the preference for family members having their own personal places, rather than it signifying wholesale family evacuations.

The Derrent family, now enjoying all mod cons at St Mabyn, recalled some colourful happenings from their farming days with great pleasure. Mrs Derrent explained, 'When we lived at St Kew Highway our farm at Little Britor had a 2-seater loo with a window. It was situated at the bottom of the yard, and was built to overhang the stream. The drop underneath was about 6 feet, which was necessary in the summer when the water flow could not cope with the build-up of solids. There were two lids and we always kept a can of neat Jeyes Fluid to pour over the heap. The worst thing was hearing the moorhens walking about underneath, and wondering if they could reach up and peck you. You could see them if you removed the lid of the second hole. This loo had two equal sized and shaped holes which we never used at the same time. I have seen 3-hole loos, with two large and one small hole. These were presumably used by nervous families who had to do everything together!'

AND YOU CAN'T SAY FAIRER THAN THAT. . .

In response to my question as to how they would sum up the old privy down the garden path, Cliff Williams, who was born and bred in Mawnan Smith, said, 'It done the job,' and his neighbour John Rickard firmly agreed, ''E done the job!'

[3]

GOING UP THE GARDEN PATH

Today Mawnan Smith has the appearance of a neat-and-tidy up-to-date village, but some of the old-timers, like Cliff Williams, recall more earthy days. 'Most of the houses in Mawnan Smith 'ad the doin's up the garden,' he said. 'You 'ad like a small wooden 'ut, like a sentry's. And of course there would've bin a wooden seat and a bucket underneath. And when the bucket was full, it was buried in the garden.' But one house occupied by a family of five had a very small garden, and when they ran out of space, it was a case of artful disposal after dark. "'Is wife would stand guard in the road,

An architectural gem at Middle Trefrew, near Camelford.

47

an' 'e used t' shout, "Is it all clear now, Mary?" And if the
coast was clear, 'e'd dash across the road with the bucket,
empty the contents in the field, an' dash back again.' This
dirty deed was usually accomplished just before old Mr
Porter emerged from the Red Lion, and came staggering up
the road. 'And 'e used t' say, "I don't know what the farmer
do put on that ther land. 'Tis some ole smell when I come up
'ere some nights!"' But the penny dropped the night he
caught them at it.

Cliff's house, built in 1922, originally had an adjoining
privy with a wooden seat and bucket underneath, and water
was obtained from a communal well in the front, from a
rainwater tank, or from the village tap. 'But we were
modernised about thirty year ago, and were glad to see the
back of the privy! The water from the well was better than we
get now.' He took me round to John Rickard's house to
admire his handsome detached privy in the back garden,
and what this hearty, forthright gentleman had to say
summed up the privy scene, past and present in an explosive
nutshell.

'Everybody 'ad one o' they, one time. An' they used t' bury
'en up 'ere in the garden, then plant the vegetables, an' eat
what they produced. 'Tis only Nature. We're too far from
Nature now, altogether. Every bugger would *die* now, if they
done such a thing, wouldn't they? What 'ave bin the change?
This is what I wanta know. 'Cos they got no immunity now,
'ave 'em? They're all bloody wimps. We've gotta Prime
Minister, an' 'e's a bloody wimp. 'E'd be 'orrified if 'e 'ad t'
bury a bucketful of shit! I should like t' watch 'en. Put 'im in
touch with reality then! All these gardens were made as full
o' shit as they could bloody well 'old! And that's the long an'
short of it. 'Cos there was nowhere else to dump 'en. You get
used t' anything. Everybody was in the same boat. You

48

oughter know that your shit never stinks. It's always other people's that do stink!'

Turning his attentions from philosophy to the finer points of the privy in question, John Rickard went on to explain, 'There was a seat across, an' a pail buggered in under. An' 'e was very elementary. You'd go in there an' let fly! It was surprisin' 'ow quick 'e got full, too. An' if you didn't shift 'en, 'e'd be over the bloody top! 'Tis pretty elementary. You didn' 'ave t' be a rocket scientist to use this. As long as you 'ad a shovel, you was all right.' John seemed to have everything at his fingertips, and apparently went on auto-pilot for nocturnal visits. 'In the middle of the night, 'twasn't so easy as 'tis now. But if you gotta go, you gotta go! It could be rainin', blowin', anythin' you like. You'd 'ave ter get out there. There wasn't no maybes about it. What the 'ell 'e wanna light t' do that for? Cover yer eyes; you couldn't miss! You knew where everything was. 'Course you did. You see, that was part o' yer life, that was. You'd know every step!'

In the days when children were expected to be seen but not heard, yet to shoulder some of the unpalatable household chores, some saw the privy at the far end of the garden as a welcome means of escape. One 80-year-old lady told me, 'By day it was a happy place to be, where one could get away for a bit; away from the others and the jobs that were my allocation, like washing the milkcan before the milkman came with his donkey cart.' She lived in a terrace of six cottages, which each had their 'sentry box' halfway down the garden, in an exposed position, close to the cliffs and the sea. 'Visiting the sentry box at night in winter was not easy. Last thing candles in lanterns were carried under cloaks or shawls, for overcoats were too difficult to manage. Horrors were inside . . . and I would pray, "Dear God, May I not sit on

This ivy covered privy is at Sworne Farm in the parish of St Martin-in-Meneage.

a snail, and protect me from the horrors outside if I tread on one." A strong wind might open the door of the privy, and all the paper would come streaming out.'

Christine Bridger, who spent twenty-five years at Rose-in-Vale, in St Kew, recalled her old double-seater with great affection. 'It was made of granite blocks with Victorian brickwork around the door. It was a beautiful building, with a slate roof and a slate floor. Outside there was a slate slab on the ground, which they used to lift up, and take out all the deposits that went into the two holes.' This had also been a setting for love, proving that double-seaters could be used in unison. 'John Cleave, who sold the place to us, said that when he got married, he and his wife used to sit there holding hands and discussing the activities of the day.'

When 91-year-old Gladys Tyack moved to her cottage in High Street, Chacewater in 1936, there was a rather novel arrangement in regard to the 3-seater privy down the garden, causing offence and more than a little embarrassment, for the wooden partition in this single building created a 2-seater for her household, and a one-seater for the family of nine next door. It was an earth closet, with the effluent dispersing into pits at the rear. 'Theirs filled up in no time, and we 'ad it all comin' in ours. So we 'ad it filled up with earth to stop that 'appenin', and 'ad a new one built. Then the next door 'ouse 'ad one, an' the next 'ouse 'ad one, so we set a trend goin' then. See, there was no water on in those days, so we couldn't 'ave any flush toilets, because we never 'ad the water.'

The shute in Shute Lane, Chacewater, where folk filled their vessels for essential household use. Gladys Tyack recalls plying between here and her home in High Street from dawn 'till dusk collecting water in pitchers to fill her tank in readiness for washday on Monday. Drinking water was delivered by horse and cart for a penny a pitcher.

Gladys's replacement privy was furnished with a bucket, which she emptied, cleaned and disinfected every day. 'My 'usband used t' dig deep pits; go down as deep as 'e could go, an' I used t' dump the bucket.' As she was so fastidious about cleanliness, and frequently scrubbed and painted the walls, no creepy crawlies stood a chance of setting up camp in Gladys's spotless privy. 'No matter what you do in life, you can always keep clean if you're ambitious t' do it. I always kept it nice, you know.'

Ruth Sanders formerly lived along the road in Shute Lane, which got its name from the mine-water shute and was once the nerve centre of the old mining village. She showed me her old privy, amongst the row of privies still lining the leafy lane, which served the cottages. 'Ours was a flush toilet, but the others had the old wooden seats. There was a galvanised jug kept in the toilet, and we used to collect water from the shute across the lane, then throw it down the toilet. You'd leave a jugful of water behind the door, ready for the next person.'

The establishment of Drift Reservoir brought mains water to Bellogas Farm at Buryas Bridge, near Penzance, in 1939, making domestic life less laborious for the Reynolds family, who have farmed there since the 1880s. Lloyd Reynolds told me of a 19th-century lady of the house who refused to have a water closet installed indoors, on grounds of hygiene. This is not so naive as it may seem, bearing in mind the hazards presented by inept plumbing at that time, and they were probably better off sticking with their proven privy, which had served them so well. This dependable little building had performed exceptional service for the very large families who have lived here, sometimes numbering twelve or thirteen. Lloyd and his daughter Stephanie chuckled to

Lloyd Reynolds and his daughter Stephanie displaying sanitary receptacles outside their farmhouse at Buryas Bridge.

recall a treasured old wedding photograph showing a hundred or so guests congregated here, and wondered how they managed after they had enjoyed a tipple. This single seater, brick-built privy with an inward opening door had a sliding bolt near floor level, which must have been a relief when it was so much in demand, saving the occupant the trouble of singing out at the sound of approaching footsteps.

Lloyd Reynolds's fastidious forbear was not alone in recoiling at the very idea of having a water closet indoors, as I discovered in a more recent tale of two privies, told to me by Keith Johnson of Lelant Downs. The farm had been in the same family for a hundred and twenty years before being modernised, and sold on several times, and the Johnsons always wondered why there was a dilapidated corrugated iron privy right at the end of the garden, and a more modern, concrete job halfway down the garden. But the riddle was solved the day the daughter of a previous owner turned up from America to wallow in nostalgia. Back in the 1950s the family farm was occupied by the remaining middle-aged brother and sister. 'She decided that she'd had enough of fetching water from a spring across the field; she decided that she wanted *indoor plumbing.* So she raised the matter somewhat dubiously with her brother – and to her amazement, he agreed! It wasn't until the plumber's work got underway, that he realised what indoor plumbing really meant. And he put his foot down, declaring "You're not doing *that* indoors". So they had to reach a compromise, with running hot and cold water and a bath indoors, and a new privy halfway down the garden. But a certain amount of progress had been achieved, for instead of having to walk fifty yards to go to the privy on a cold, wet, windy night, she only had to walk twenty-five yards!'

Mrs Derrent told me about her former privy at St Kew Highway: 'The privy was well down below the farmhouse. It was quite tall when you got in, but there was a low lintel, and you had to duck down very low as you made an exit, because there was a step. I mean, I've banged my head on it heaps of times. If you didn't remember – bang!'

Like many other farms, they diversified by taking in visitors keen to experience the delights of rural life. 'When we did Bed and Breakfast, one of the worst things was seeing them holding their heads as they came back up the yard in the mornings. Why do tourists never read "Mind your head" notices? We had to keep pots under the beds for night-time as it was a long way to go from the house. We always told our B & Bs about the loo before they booked, and most of the guests thought it was quaint.

'Just before we had an indoor loo fitted, a friend came to lodge with us, which was unexpected, and caused him a few problems. My husband had decided that as our loo would soon be ready, he would put up a fence for the pigs in front of the soon-to-be-redundant outside loo. This fence directly crossed the path to the loo, and upset our friend who had an office job and had to look smart in the morning. It was very difficult to get over the wire fence without getting stuck in the mud – and fending off the pigs at the same time! The last time I looked into this loo was after a flood, when the water ran down the farmtrack and reached a level at least three inches above the holes.'

This wasn't the only privy known to Mrs Derrent. 'Our second farm, Trevilnick, at Helman Tor, had an outside earth closet, which we never had to use, and there was also the ruin of one below the ruins of the old house. This old toilet was rumoured to have contaminated the well, and all the people living in the farmhouse died of typhoid. So that's why they built the new house. Needless to say we never used the old well in the wash-house. Another loo that I used was at Hingham Mill, near Sladesbridge. It was next to the mill and over the mill leat. This loo had to be used with care, and you had to ensure that the mill was not working, with the water from the mill leat being used to turn the mill wheel. If the wheel was turning, anything in the mill leat went around on the wheel!'

'In the 1930s, I lived in a block of five terraced cottages which 'ad only two stone-built toilets,' Jack Harding of Menheniot, near Liskeard, told me. 'Then the estate of Coldrenick built three galvanised things, like sentry boxes. There was no back doors to these terraced cottages in those days. You'd 'ave to go a mile around and what seemed like a mile down to the end of the garden. As a boy I can remember sitting in the privy, the massive great cobwebs, and the flies flyin' around, attracted by the smell and everything. They would pitch into the reservoir, and out would come massive great spiders to kill the flies.'

Jack's wife Rosemarie had similar childhood experiences at Trethevy, near Darite, on the edge of Bodmin Moor. 'To reach the privy we 'ad to open a garden gate and go up a path, past the gooseberry bushes, until we came to the galvanised building in the next garden. On a winter's evening you'd 'ave a coat over your 'ead, an' run like anything to get there, and it was dark inside the privy. I wouldn't like to go back to those days again. We are very fortunate today to pull the chain and have instant running water.' Jack pointed out that they were all in the same boat, and cited the experience of an 80-year-old friend. 'This lady, livin' at Merrymeet, where 'er was born, remembers goin' out to the privy with a candle, an' shoo-in' off the rats an' everythin'!' He chuckled, then came out with a privy classic, which has stood the test of time. 'There was a story goin' around that a lady on holiday from upcountry went down to the privy, an' protested that there was no lock on the door. "Oh, that's all right," said the owner, "Don't worry; we've never 'ad a bucket pinched yet!"'

[4]

IT HAD TO GO SOMEWHERE!

'The WC is really one of the conveniences that really is good. You just pull the handle – and it's gone! Everything just disappears; you don't see it. That's marvellous!' Simon Perry, who had lived at many places, including Hendra Cottage near Mitchell, was in no doubt that things had improved, but then, as one of the offspring of rather eccentric parents, it had often fallen to his lot to empty the privy. 'I used to hate this job. I didn't mind digging the holes – it was emptying the damn bucket afterwards.' I made the remark that this seemed rather tough for a child of the family, and he agreed. 'It *was* tough. For a start, digging holes in the woods was tough, because of all the roots. I liked to try and dig a *big* hole, so that it would last a month or so. They were normally huge great buckets. Great big galvanised buckets; about four gallons, I would say. When that was full it was really bad. Occasionally they could afford the chemical stuff, but mostly there was no chemical stuff, and it did stink terrible! Quite honestly, as a child and as a teenager, I would rather go out in the woods to spend a penny than go in the privy.'

John Hopkins at Summercourt remembered the bucket-type privy very well. 'Dad had some fields at the back of a row of cottages, and one old chap, who did his garden regularly, never bothered to cover up. He just tipped the bucket on top. One day when Dad was working close by, he saw flies all over the place. So he asked this old chap why he didn't cover it up, pointing out that flies went from there and settled on your food. And the old boy says, "I don't give a bugger where

Margaret Ball of Lanner with her granny's chamber pot.

they settle," 'e says, "I'm eighty seven, an' it don't matter t'me now!"

'Father liked raspberries. Father had so much to do on the farm that he didn't get much time for gardening, and his raspberries didn't do so well. Further down the row of cottages was a chap who grew very good raspberries. When Father asked him why his raspberries were so much better than ours, the answer was, "I soak 'en well!"' I had often heard about organic rhubarb, so this was a new one to add to the privy repertoire. John went on to tell me that one advantage of having a primitive privy was that his wife gained a place in hospital for the birth of their eldest son. 'They didn't want her having a baby at home – with those facilities,' he chuckled.

The country custom of tipping the bucket may not have been immortalised by poets and minstrels, but nevertheless young love blossomed in the earthy context. For Plymouth-born Gloria Stephens met her husband at Penhale Farm near Lanivet when they were teenagers, and every now and again their time together was punctuated by his being required to go and dig a hole in the garden. She eventually realised that this was where he emptied the contents of the family privy bucket. 'I remember very clearly this huge great pit in the garden, where wonderful fruit and vegetables grew.'

'We 'ad a long garden an' grew large rhubarb outside the privy,' Jack Harding told me. 'It was all newspapers in those days, an' when you ran out of newspaper, you used rhubarb leaves to wipe yer be'ind. You always 'ad a laugh, 'cos you'd always see one of the neighbours diggin' a pit durin' the day. You'd 'ave these great galvanised buckets, and always under cover of darkness you'd go an' dump them. You'd take different places in the garden durin' the year. Sometimes you'd be diggin' up newspaper an' stuff like that, where it 'adn't properly rotted down, but nobody died in those days. All the rhubarb an' that, it was massive. There was an Irish couple who lived down from us. 'E used to throw 'is slop pail of urine over 'is cabbages, an' 'e 'ad massive great cabbages. An' 'e said to Mother, "Look, 'elp yourself to a cabbage," 'e said. "No thank you," said Mother. "I don't want any!" I mean, nobody died in those days. Everybody was more 'ealthy.'

Frank Kneebone's 2-seater on his former smallholding at Polgooth, however, seemed to empty itself. 'It was out in the yard, and basically, when it needed cleaning we just pushed it out through a hole in the back, and left it there. Nobody ever cleaned it at all, as far as I am aware. It just sort of dispersed. Just as you had a dungheap on a farm, well, you had a human dung heap. With these 2-seaters, one seat was often smaller than the other. The one with the smaller diameter was for the younger members of the family to use, because they'd got smaller bottoms. Otherwise they might disappear down the hole. So these were not necessarily for side-by-side sitting. We got our water from a shute, which was literally a hole in the hedge with a spring coming out. And in the summertime, when the water level's lower, we made sure that we didn't have any water that the cattle had soiled. We went further up the field and got it in the woods, where the cattle weren't. You found many privies built straight over the rivers, so anyone living lower down had to take pot-luck. Then again, when you lived in the country, you got used to all these things. In some ways I think we live too clean today.'

Margaret Ball's late husband Albert would have been delighted at the concept of a self-emptying privy. But in the meantime this reluctant tipper of the bucket resorted to procrastination. 'The tales I could tell about tippin' the bucket is no man's business,' laughed this jolly lady. 'I used to say, "Albert, 'ave you tipped the bucket?" "No, but I'll do it when I come 'ome." Well, 'e'd come 'ome an' sit down after workin' all day. Then I'd be sayin' "Ave you done that bucket?" "No, I'll do it in the mornin'." When the mornin' was come it was "No, I'll do it tonight. I can't stay now. . ." An' so 'twould go on. An' in the end I 'ad t' do it myself! An' 'twas the devil's own job to dig that pit to tip the bucket. 'Twas really awful. I wouldn' wish it on anybody!'

BUCKETS AND PEARLS

I was introduced to a recycled bucket on my visit to Trewinnion Farm. 'I remember using this one day, for carrying corn to the calves,' David Hopkins laughed, 'and Dad said to me, "Do you know what that was originally? It's an old shit bucket!"'

Anne Thomas, who was brought up on Trewince Farm at St Issey, recalled the receptacle that she was far too polite to call a shit bucket, and said that it was the job of the farm workers to empty them. 'They were a special shape, these privy buckets; they had a double lip and a handle. You used to see the remains of these old buckets lying around all over the place. It was primitive, to be sure, but they weren't smelly, you know, if they were properly emptied, and it was wonderful on the garden. Then my mother had an Elsan put in. That was the next step on. The Elsan had chemicals in, and was easier for emptying.'

Lerryn, south-east of Lostwithiel, has a profusion of engaging privies, pigsties and linneys in the vicinity of Piggy Lane, some of which have virtually disappeared beneath a mantle of ivy, much to the delight of the wildlife. Indeed, I

A gem of a privy at Trewinnion Farm, Summercourt, which is a 2-seater earth closet. The 'shit bucket' in the foreground saw service elsewhere, and is now put to general use around the farm.

A profusion of privies in Lerryn.

had to beware of low-flying, late-nesting swallows, as I was escorted around by George Mansell and his cat on a sunny September day. 'All the privies along here had buckets, and when it became dark people would take them down to The Dock to empty them. Everything would be taken away on the out-going tide. That was the principle of the sewage system here, and it was discreetly done at night.' Ernie Mitchell, who has lived in a cottage adjoining The Dock since 1949, also knew all about the nocturnal custom of emptying the buckets. 'When the tide was up, late at night, you could hear all the people going by with their buckets. That went on 'till 1971. Then, lo and behold! We had the sewage plant put in, and everybody went flush!'

Generations of country folk conditioned to the hard toil of everyday life, took things in their stride. Mrs Minna Segrave of Tregenna in Blisland had an earth closet at the end of her flowery garden path, which emptied into a field beyond, and had to be cleaned out periodically. However, when she was a centenarian, she made use of a slop bucket with a lid, and paid young Margaret Long a penny a week to empty it every day. 'I used to call the slop pail the Mail Coach,' laughed Margaret Parkyn. 'I had to shovel earth and ashes from a box on to the contents of the pail. I felt quite rich earning one penny per week, and if I saved up for two weeks, I had great spending power. I remember buying a string of pearls from Miss Riches' shop for tuppence.'

Of course, if there was running water it was a real bonus for privy builders – a running stream was *most* convenient!

I was told of children in Lerryn who revelled in crossing the river to the St Winnow side at low tide to play with a little girl in the big house, where an ancient privy in the orchard overhung the river. No trip was complete without a visit to this excitingly positioned privy, to gain noisy and spectacular relief from on high, whatever the state of the tide.

Robin Moore of Trefrew Farm, near Camelford, spent part of the war at his great aunt's home at Trethevey between Tintagel and Boscastle. Although the house had all mod cons, it was far more alluring to cross the road and use the picturesque old privy in the kitchen garden, where celery, rhubarb and other vegetables grew to perfection. 'It had been built above a small but fast-flowing stream by the boundary hedge, so it was automatically and continually flushed. Like many of these privies, it had a very substantial full width seat, with plenty of room on either side. Many a peaceful moment was spent residing there in contemplation, or the reading of the written word.'

Those who were able to harness natural watercourses in

This pretty privy positioned over a stream at Trethevey, near Boscastle, has fond childhood associations for Robin Moore.

this way thought that they were on to a good thing. It was a case of being out of sight and out of mind, and it took the backache out of emptying the privy. Eighty-two-year-old Howard Tamblyn, now living in Callington, cast his mind back to the idyllic days of childhood at Pillaton, where all things were bright and beautiful. '"The tall trees in the forest . . . the meadows where we play . . . the rushes by the water, we gather every day. . ." Well, we had it all. I was reared in a large dower house near a mill leat, and just below the house was a stream where the rushes grew. Water was brought from the leat to the house by an iron pipe. This supplied an old water closet, and the effluent drained into the overflow from the mill leat into the river in the valley. Part of the overflow from the water wheel ran underground, and a shed was built over this underground overflow. One sat on a seat with a hole

65

in it, and the excreta dropped into the water which ran down the overflow to the river. You'd hear it drop. And sometimes you'd hear a rat down there, running around.'

Justin Brooke of Marazion told me that it was customary in the china clay districts to site the privy over a leat, such as the one that ran from the Treffry Viaduct in Luxulyan and down the north slope of the valley to a china clay works at Pont's Mill. He and the late Cyril Noall, the St Ives historian, found a similar situation at Geevor tin mine which they visited after it closed. A solidly-built privy bridged the stream running down to the sea into which all the mine's waste water was channelled.

The sanitary situation in rural Cornwall must have been a shock to the American servicemen, who arrived in these parts around 1944. 'I s'pose they thought we was a bit be'ind the times,' mused Jack Harding of Menheniot. 'They 'ad a filtration plant at Round'ouse, which used to filtrate water from the River Seaton. They 'ad about twenty bowsers, which supplied all the American forces, right down to Falmouth and to the Tavistock moors; everywhere where the American forces was congregated for the D-Day landings. There wasn't any water supply then, I mean, this village 'ad standpipes right up to the mid 1950s. About 'alf a mile upstream from this filtration plant at a place called Factory, the locals were doin' their business over the stream which ran into it. They 'ad privies over' angin' the stream. But the Americans thought that what they were puttin' in would kill off anything.'

MEMORIES FROM PENRYN . . .

In 1970 Bucket an' Chuckit was still the order of the day for most of the households of Penryn, according to Eric

Dawkins, of Penryn Town Council. 'The buckets were in outhouses, and they were chemical closets,' he explained. 'If there was a convenient manhole or anything, the contents were deposited there, or in the outer fringes it was spread on the adjacent land and fields . . . Oh yes, there are still quite a few people around who can remember those days!'

. . . AND WADEBRIDGE

Brian Tooze, who was brought up in Egloshayle Road in the 1930s remembered, 'There were five privies in a row, for the five cottages by the river, and we used to have to go the length of the garden. We flushed our toilet by throwing down a bucketful of water . . . But it was all up-graded, and we had a washstand put in and connected into the main drain. The river was not far away, and it was all piped into the river.

'When I was a boy, Wadebridge was a *boat* river. It was always timber boats and coal boats and flour boats. And as youngsters we grew up swimming in the river. Diving off into the river and going to all the local beaches.' He paused to reflect on what they had been swimming in, and I made some remark about it being more a case of going through the motions. 'We literally swam in sewage, but the tides used to come up and go back and take it away, you see. And I can't honestly remember anyone suffered any problems or died on account of swimming in the river. I know a lot of people still living, from my swimming days, and I'm seventy next year. So it's quite amazing, really. And that came from all kinds of toilets, from wood type toilets, wash down toilets and the waste from the boats.'

This renovated privy belongs to the famous, pillared Keigwin House, which is the oldest house in Mousehole. It is attached to another building and may originally have served several households.

. . . AND MOUSEHOLE

Peter Pearman, a local fisherman for many years, can recall life in Mousehole in the 1950s. 'It was quite common to see people walk down to the quay with their nightly slop pails, which they emptied over the side of the quay.' There were traditional rivalries between the Up-alongers and Down-alongers of Mousehole, which were forgotten in confrontations with the folk of Penzance and Newlyn, and insults flew in all directions. 'Newlyn people were called Newlyn Buckets. They were said to bear the marks of privy buckets on their bottoms, on account of being the last people to use the old bucket toilets, which were emptied when a big lorry came around.'

YER OWN BACK!

Many colourful tales are told about the old 'honey carts' which perambulated around the Cornish streets in olden times, but none more entertaining than those surrounding Mr Brunyee of Padstow. "E 'ad a 'orse an' cart an' 'twas called the Mornin' Star,' explained Margaret Ball. 'An' 'e used t' go to the 'ouses an' cottages, an' collect the muck from the privies, an' put it in the cart; mix 'en with ashes an' take 'en away. An' one of those days 'e 'ad an accident with 'en, an' upset it all. The chain broke, an' all the muck washed down the 'ill. An' 'e said that the people where 'e'd been must come out an' clear it all up. "You've all gotta come out an' gather up yer own!" 'e said.'

[5]

SOME LADIES AND THEIR PRIVIES

'Aunt Dorothy was a very down-to-earth, strict and no-nonsense sort of person,' confided Jean Sewart, telling me about her aunt who lived in Treneague, near Wadebridge, in the 1940s. 'Rather overpowering for me as a youngster sent to live with her during the war, but a woman ahead of her time. She lived in a cottage in the woods, which later became a nature reserve. As there was no privy in the cottage, she built one over a stream. It was just a wooden hut over the stream with a sort of felted roof with a tar coating. It was bread-and-butter sort of planks overlapping, just like an ordinary garden shed. The arrangement inside was a drainpipe slotted into a hole in the floor, with a wooden seat resting on the top. So it discharged straight into the stream. The water was tapped above the stream with a big pipe, and then it ran into the bath. You could turn the taps on, and then it ran back into the stream when you pulled the plug out. It was all very ingenious and very effective, but not very hygienic for the people living in Wadebridge.

'When my aunt built on to the cottage, she turned the old privy into a shed, and called it the Garden Room. You were never allowed to mention the fact that it had once been a privy. I think she was rather ashamed of it after she became environmentally conscious, and rather regretted that she had built this privy polluting a stream. But this is the way it would have been in those days, during the Second World War.

'On a nearby farm lived Miss Bate, with her father, mother and brother. Their privy was a three or four holer, with chickens under the same roof. So you sat there and opposite you would be the nestboxes, with the chickens laying or brooding their eggs or something.' Could this be my opportunity to find the answer to the perennial question: 'When there were these multiple holers, would the family sit in a row?' I ventured to ask. 'I don't know,' said Jean, adding on reflection, 'but why would they have them otherwise? On one occasion Aunt Dorothy went up to the farm and found Miss Bate fussing around prior to a visit to Wadebridge. She was getting in a panic, and asked Aunt Dorothy if she happened to have a safety pin, explaining, "I always put a safety pin in me drawers before I go to town, in case they fall down!"'

Derek Thomas, who was brought up in Wadebridge, had always felt overawed by a dignified and rather haughty lady from farming circles, called Mrs Phillips. When he was a schoolboy in the early part of the war, he had to go around distributing leaflets encouraging people to collect hips and haws from the hedgerows for their Vitamin C content. To save time he usually went round to the back of the houses, opened the door and tossed the circulars inside. On one occasion he came upon a green door with serrated edges, which he took to be the back door, and pushed it open – only to find himself staring straight into the eyes of the elderly and stately Mrs Phillips, enthroned on the outside privy. 'What do you think you're doing?' demanded the startled lady. He muttered some sort of apology, and had the presence of mind to toss a leaflet inside, closing the door behind him. 'Ever since then, I've been very cautious of doors at the back of houses with serrated edges!' Their eyes met when they bumped into each other in Wadebridge a few days later, but wisely, she walked on without comment, as if nothing had happened.

[6]

THOSE WERE THE DAYS

Eric Mildren of Sithney was to become something of a connoisseur of privy-lore, on account of his father being a carpenter, wheelwright and undertaker at Nancegollen, willing to turn his hand to the repair and maintenance of privies. On one occasion he was asked to make a privy to dimensions given by the landlord of a farm. 'This was made up in the workshop with a 3" x 2" (75mm x 50mm) timber frame, covered back, sides and roof with corrugated galvanised iron, and with a door in the front opening out. Inside would be a wooden box to cover the bucket, and the hinged top would have a round hole cut in it (for obvious reasons), and with a circular cover. I accompanied my father one Saturday morning when the privy was delivered and set up at the rear of the farmhouse. On seeing the privy the tenant farmer was none too pleased, and I heard him say, "That's no b..... good! It's so small that you'd 'ave t' undress outside, an' backen in!"'

On another occasion his father was asked to make a new seat for an outside privy. 'Because timber was scarce and on ration at the time, he used a plank of elm, which had been set aside for his wheelwrighting activities. I expect it came from a local tree which had blown down, or was cut down, and had been sawn into different thickness planks, ready for use in the future. When the job was complete, the lady of the house said that she would not use it, as it looked too much like a coffin lid!'

'Did they really use that . . .?' Alice Bryant takes a photo call inside the old two-seater privy on her grandparents' farm.

All sorts of interesting bits and pieces were recycled in the making and repair of privies. Peggy Pearce of Falmouth told me of a particularly striking example of this, on her grandparents' farm near Perranwell, and also captured the essence of childhood when she told me, 'Last thing at night I would run down the long path, rattling the corrugated sheet wall of the barn with a stick, to scare off anything that may be lurking in the darkness. At the end was the privy; a little room with white walls and a green door. It had a bench on two levels; the higher one for grown ups and a low one for the children. It was a long drop to the floor below, so no odour was ever present! I can remember peering down the hole, wondering who's done this? And who's done that! My cousin fell down the hole on one occasion.

'By night I hated to go there, but by day it held a magic for me because the little window on a level with the children's privy was of stained glass. My world could be changed as I pressed my nose to the various glass panels. A red world could become a yellow one; then a blue world. The plum tree beyond would change as I moved my head. I wonder why it had this lovely window? Was it made from left over glass from the landing window in the main house? Who knows? But for a child it was a delight, and I still love stained glass to this day. I am sure the window influenced my life, as I became an artist, and colour is so important to me.'

Leonard Masters, now of Penrose near Padstow, has a childhood memory of some portable wooden privies, introduced by an enterprising local carpenter, which were rather too easy to move around. They were of tongue and groove construction, tarred, with galvanised roofs, and outward opening doors because of the limited space. Like other privies in the area, any locking arrangement would

Peggy Pearce's interpretation of her grandparents' privy, which was a source of fascination to her.

have utilised part of an old gin trap. On one occasion a lady was trotting down the garden sighing for relief, when she suddenly realised that her privy had vanished without trace. The shed, bucket and all was later discovered in the middle of a 14 acre field, having been carried off by some high spirited young men of the village, who were wont to enjoy such pranks. Leonard remembered seeing the rotting remains of these portable privies for years afterwards. Although they may have been versatile, they had not withstood the test of time as their traditionally constructed counterparts did.

It paid not to linger too long in the less substantially built privies, especially in windy areas like the Tamar Valley. In some cases they were attached to the 'linney', which was the name given to the wash-house around these parts. The inevitable happened to the rickety, old privy in Mavis Harris's childhood garden at Tutwell, in Stoke Climsland parish in the 1930s. 'I can see it now,' she said. 'It was a very windy day, and it was getting a bit shaky on its foundations. We were looking out of the window and saw it go over like a pack of cards! So they gathered up the debris and had to make use of the old slop bucket under the stairs, until the landlord sent a carpenter along to fashion a new privy.

Yvonne King told me of her childhood home in Luckett, on the hillside overlooking some of the cottages and their privies, inconveniently set at some distance amongst lanes and gardens, and not very private. As children they used to run in and out of the drangways, much to the annoyance of the cottagers, who came out and chased them away. When the privy of one disagreeable old couple blew over during a storm, the children were disappointed to find that it was unoccupied at the time.

Dermont Richards recalled other childhood high jinks involving his family's wooden privy at the bottom of the garden. This had a couple of slats missing at the back. 'My Granny used to come and visit us once a fortnight and when she went to the loo, us children would go down and sting her behind with stinging nettles. When Father came in from the fields she would say "Cyril, it's about time you cut down those stinging nettles." Father would smile and say, "Yes, Mother." He knew what we'd been up to. Later on in the '50s we had the Elsan toilets, very up-market, and toilet rolls, but it wasn't the same somehow.'

Hilda Bennett of Penrose talked to me of fecund gardens and chamber pots. A profusion of vegetables was needed to feed hungry mouths (she was one of ten children) and perpetuated a constant recycling process. 'We grew everything; parsnips an' carrots an' lovely green cabbages. They used t' tip the bucket on the garden, and water the cabbages with the slops from upstairs. Marvellous cabbages. Well, 'twas ammonia, wasn't it?' Thoughts of chamber pots reminded Hilda of her Victorian-style father, who was very strict with the children if a trifle self-indulgent, as befitted the head of the household. The children used a chamber pot upstairs, and after he'd been on the beer, he often had to resort to it in the middle of the night. When the level came up to his thumb, he knew it was full, and was obliged to empty it out of the window. On one occasion, when accumulated candle grease set the lantern on fire, he managed to extinguish it by dunking it in the brimming chamber pot. The contents of the chamber pot were transferred to the slop pails, then brought downstairs and disposed of in the garden.

Hilda Bennett outside her delightful privy.

As a child Gloria Stephens used to visit an aunt who lived on a Bodmin estate. 'The toilet was down a set of winding stairs that went down to the underground kitchen. You went out the door into a huge courtyard, with a high wall, and at the far end there was one long row of toilets, with separate little doors for each individual house. Inside was a wooden seat with a wooden frame. I remember sitting down on this little wooden bench with a hole in it. Most undignified, of course, having come from Plymouth, with large, airy rooms with plenty of light, and indoor toilets. The kitchen was like the black hole of Calcutta; as dark as a dungeon. Going across this huge courtyard at night, and sitting on this little wooden bench was something that stuck in your mind. Lighting? Oh, no! Nothing like that! If you went down there at night you were in real trouble. You took a torch with you, and you didn't hang about.'

An old friend of mine in Falmouth, Jeanette, also has vivid memories of the night-time trip to the privy. 'I used to run down the back garden into the loo after dark, always leaving the door ajar. Then I would run back indoors. There was no light, and it was eerie. I probably saw the moon from the seat of the loo, more than from anywhere else. It was a comfort, because it was the only light. My fondness for the night sky may well stem from the early days of sitting on the outside loo. I didn't leave the door ajar in the daytime, because I had to preserve propriety.'

Unpleasant nocturnal surprises were not so likely to befall the members of Valerie Grigg's family at Higher North Country, on account of her father's forethought. 'We had two toilets, semi-detached as you might say. They were red brick and very posh. There was a little path across the front of them, and a pink climbing rose at the other side of the path. The toilets had a wooden surround with a wooden cover with a handle, and was connected to a cesspit which led under the field hedge and drained into the field. Inside the toilet house was painted white and there was a stone ledge up over the door, where my father lit a tiny green-painted tin lamp and placed it in the evenings, so that we would be able to see any spiders.'

LITERARY (AND OTHER) MEMOIRS

Terry Beer of Carlyon Bay, who was a choirboy at Tywardreath about 45 years ago came up with a fascinating anecdote with a literary slant. 'We used to to go Tregaminion chapel once a month, to keep it consecrated. The vicar would take four or five of the choirboys down there, for a short service of dedication. We then went down to Menabilly House, where we had tea with the du Mauriers. I can remember one huge room, where there was the biggest rocking horse I've ever seen. The French doors from this room were open, and we went out into the garden and found a well built, detached structure. We went and had a look, and inside was this huge plank of wood, with two holes cut in it. There was a hole down below. I don't know how deep it was; I didn't delve that far. We didn't use it because we were afraid we might fall in! But it was a side-by-side wooden structure, and obviously in use at that time.'

The literary and contemplative theme turns up in various guises. Josephine Sweet remembers the old closet in a galvanised building at the top of her childhood garden at Carnon Mine, where they also had a bomb shelter. For her it was a seat of learning, not to mention a means of escaping the washing up. 'You would have the newspaper hung there. The thing is, it was usually the *News of the World*, which I wasn't allowed to read. Then if you forgot to take a book with you, you'd start to read it, and you couldn't find the other piece, because it was hung up on a piece of string on a rail.'

Which reminds me, Leonard Masters said something about the *Western Morning News* being a particularly good newspaper, but I'm not quite sure what he meant.

[7]

IN THE PLAYGROUND

While traditional village schools may have been firm on discipline and thorough in the teaching of the three Rs, the situation of the privies in the playground left much to be desired in terms of hygiene and social training. These humble little outbuildings housed earth, bucket or trough arrangements, which could be communal or individual, giving rise to a secret culture far removed from the constraints of the classroom.

Carrie Ham, who attended school in the 1920s, recalled, 'There were two yards; one for the boys an' one for the girls, an' each 'ad its own privy. The one for the girls was in a li'le 'ouse down in the corner, an' there was a bucket business. An' every week the caretaker's son would come up an' empty these 'ere buckets. 'E would take them down an' throw them in the stream. 'E always used t' do that fer yearz an' yearz. Sidney, 'e was called. Sidney used t' come an' empty the buckets when 'is mother was cleanin' the school. I c'n remember that, as well as c'n be.'

Eighty-three-year-old Margaret Ball, who attended St Eval school, could also remember some finer details. 'There was a toilet down be'ind the school. An' there was a little door at the back, where they used t' pull the pail out from the toilet an' tip 'en on the field. The school caretaker used t' do it. Lily Sowden, that was. She was the cleaner an' school caretaker, an' she used t' 'ave t' do this beastly job.'

Mavis Harris told me, 'I went to Luckett school, and the privy was quite convenient. You just came out of the door and

The old privies at Stoke Climsland school looking rather forlorn.

The former privies at St Day school now serve as useful storage space.

it was a few yards away. There were three little ones, just children's height, and there was one for the teacher. So there were four on the girls' side, and presumably the boys were the same. The school was closed, and we went to Callington just before the war started. They had flush loos, but we had to go right across the school playground, and we took a dim view of that. Specially if it was raining.'

Diana Horner, now of Callington, a walking encyclopaedia of privy culture, discovered that 'when they built the present primary school at Upton Cross, they had the privies along the back wall, which opened on to a field, which was also part of the school property. They had gardens over there and on a Friday night, I think it was, the senior boys had to go and empty the privies in a pit or something, somewhere near the allotments. The girls were obviously spared this job. There were little trapdoors at the back, apparently, that would be pulled out to empty the contents.'

Leila Facey used to walk from Talvan Farm to the village school at Lanreath. 'Of course there were outside toilets at the school, which you sort of visited, but left as quickly as you could because of the smell and suchlike. Across the playground there were what we called the Boys' Round and the Girls' Round. We used to say, "I'm going to the Girls' Round," or the boys would be going to the Boys' Round. Whether that was because of the round seats cut into the wooden tops, I don't know. There was this little building behind a wall, which was much the size of a pigsty, really. And I think there were two or three different compartments with one seat in each of them. There was one door to each compartment. The Boys' Round was a separate building at the other side of the school. I don't know what happened at the Boys' Round, beause the girls weren't allowed to go up there. I think there was a toilet slightly more modern in a different building. Perhaps that was the teachers' one.'

The stench of the school privy also made a lasting impression on Mary Littleton. 'The lavatory at St Neot school! It was years before they had a proper one. There was a row of four in the girls', and they used to stink to high heaven! They were like a round drainpipe, only bigger than a drainpipe, with round seats on the top. This was around the back of the school.' I heard tales of children putting their mid-morning lunch treats on the communal seats beside them, as they used the privy, and of the horrible sight of the effluent before it was flushed out.

Flats now occupy the site of the old village school in Mawnan Smith, near the Methodist chapel, where Cliff Williams received his education in the 1930s. 'There was about nineteen children when I was goin' t' school, an' what we 'ad, regards sanitation, was in the playground, a bit away from the school. An' you 'ad the girls' doin's and the boys'. 'Twas a detached building, like a hut, more or less, an' I think 'twas in stone, with a door. I don't think there were any bolts on the door; just a latch. No locks, nor nothin', no. An' what it was, was wood seats in each, just goin' along. One seat in each. There was nothin' underneath, you know. Everythin' just dropped right down. There was a partition, of course, from the boys' and girls'. You just went in an' you sat on the doin's an' that for the necessary. An' every so often the man who 'ad the 'ouse an' garden across the way, used t' clear out the toilets. 'E put it in a barrow an' took it to 'is garden. 'E grew great stuff in 'is garden; lovely rhubarb an' such like. 'E grew all sorts in there. Yeah. Everyone admired 'is garden.'

Viv Pentecost attended the little school at Mabe in the 1930s. 'The boys' and girls' toilets were of stone construction, separated by a wall. They were individual compartments with fairly small wood seats. Periodically the caretaker cleaned out the toilets from a rear access, rather like a trapdoor. He used to scoop it out once a week. The boys' urinal was a slate enclosure with a walk-in entrance, and a lead trough going into a soakaway. There were no flush facilities at all, in either situation.'

Supply teacher Enid Lydiatt gives an engaging insight into the sanitary situation at St Ewe school in 1963. 'It was wintertime and I was told to report for duty. I didn't realise that I was going to have such an enjoyable and interesting time. The caretaker welcomed me, everything was spotlessly clean. As there was no mains water anywhere (a fact I didn't discover until much later), the water came from a huge granite tank in the playground, roughly ten feet high. The lavatories, of course, at the end of the yard were unbelievable – the walls and floor were spotless, but to my amazement the wooden seats were 'U' shaped, supported over a coalscuttle with a small handmade footstool in front. At the back of the seat was a wooden box, the size of a small suitcase with a lid on top. This was filled in summer with earth, and ashes in the winter. After finishing you gave the box a sharp blow with your elbow, and the contents shot into the coalscuttle.'

[8]

Creepy Crawlies And Other Hazards

The many hazards of privy life were recalled with much hilarity during a coffee morning at Brea Chapel. Christine Martin remembered how brave one had to be to visit her childhood privy at Rosewarne Downs, on account of a cockerel being its self-appointed guardian. 'We 'ad a big rooster, an' 'e used t' chase us around the garden. An' if 'e saw us go in, 'e'd be outside, waitin'. If we were gone too long, Mother would wonder what was 'appenin', an' would come an' chase 'im away. 'E used t' more or less keep an eye on the place.' The talk became quite animated and laughter

Up the garden path at Lelant Downs. This privy is still in daily use.

filled the air, as folk exchanged tales about rhubarb, buckets and spiders, newspapers and candles, Jeyes Fluid and rats, in the days when you walked down the old garden path, and everyone knew where you were going: 'The blinkin' rats! You used t' bang everythin' before you'd go in!' and '*Great big* spiders, they were. The cobwebs were the strongest things goin'. If you went down at night, they'd get in your hair, and you'd 'ave to brush it out in the morning.' And the Minister brought the house down when he told us of another sort of privy problem: 'My grandmother got stuck in the privy when she went to visit friends. The loo was small and she was rather big, and she couldn't get out. So they all came along and pulled her out!'

Stories of creepy crawlies and uncomfortable encounters with wildlife cropped up all over the county. John Thurstans of St Buryan told me of his first encounter with a privy, in 1942: '. . . quite an experience. An expedition. You left the cottage through a gate at the side and entered a paddock patrolled by a stroppy cockerel. Then, along a short path to a wooden shed built over a nettle-filled ditch. Once inside you had to climb onto a big wooden box-like affair with a large circular hole cut in the top. I peered down into the forbidding gloom and sensed a faint "essence of rhino" wafting up. The hole was adult size and I had to cling fiercely to the top to avoid plummeting to an unspeakable fate. Suddenly, in mid-performance, if I can put it so delicately, I heard a sound. "Slip slop, slip slap, puck puck, slip slop." It was getting nearer. Something was coming along the ditch! It was not in my vocabulary at the time but "shit scared" comes to my mind. I dropped a chunk of toilet paper down the hole and the farm cockerel, for it was he, let out a fiendish squawk of horror. I yelled at the top of my voice. People came running as I fled from the hut with my shorts around my ankles.'

Some of the cosier privies often found favour with pets and farm animals, as places of refuge. Joan Vaas had memories of goats: 'When they had babies, the little kids were attracted to the old privy, as the floor made a nice shelter for them. So you might go rushing out there, only to find a little kid had got there before you!'

Eric Mildren's recollection of farm privies is less appealing. One day while visiting his grandfather at Wheal Vor, near Breage, he was sitting on the privy and had the misfortune to be stung by a little busy bee, apparently on the look-out for a novel way to improve the shining hour.

And, oh yes, the spiders – they were everywhere, though perhaps never quite as terrifying as the ones described over the breakfast table to Allison Randlesome (from appropriately

When the Elliott family first moved to the 17th-century cottage, to which this privy is attached, a resident mouse would appear on the rotting lintel above the door to wash its face and keep an eye on the proceedings when it was being used. (Photo by John Elliott)

named Jolly's Bottom, near Chacewater) by her older brothers and sisters when she was a little girl. They took pleasure in telling her '. . . tales of spiders creeping menacingly around the rim of the bucket on which they sat, spiders so big that you could not hold them in two hands, even had you the desire to do so!'

Spiders in the childhood privy apparently held no terrors for Margaret Ball, but mice and moleskins did. 'If I saw a mouse, I'd jump for miles. They used to catch moles in those days and dry and sell the skins for a few pennies each. They'd skin them and hang them out to dry on the inside wooden walls of the privy. My sister used to make me touch them, and I was terrified because 'twas furry. She'd take my hand and put it on the furs, and I couldn't abide it. I used to run away.'

Hazards came in all shapes and sizes, particularly for the unwary. Yvonne King told me of a privy in her village which had found favour with a cat: 'The occupant of one of the cottages worked for the Duke of Bedford at Endsleigh, and he had to leave very early in the morning to cycle to his work. He always visited the outside closet, which just had a wooden bench seat over a bucket, in the dark. One day his next door neighbours wondered what all the swearing was about, and it turned out that he had dropped his pipe on the seat, where Pussy had left a present!' No doubt he took a lantern with him after that.

Night-time and 'the dark' featured in most people's childhood memories. Hilda Bennett was adamant that they did not worry about uncomfortable weather conditions, having never known anything different, but did admit that nocturnal adventures could be a trifle daunting at times. 'You might go out in the dark with a candle or hurricane lantern, get 'alfway there. . . The candle blow out. . . You've lost yer matches, an' you find yerself in the cabbage bed, or somethin'! There was no lights of any kind; the only light you got, was the moon. There was spiders an' cobwebs 'angin' down, and you'd be afraid of you life there was a rat, or somethin'. You'd 'ear scratchin' an' that, an' you're sayin' there's a rat climbin' up be'ind the bucket. And you'd gotta be careful you don't get a nip!'

Steve Collins disliked using his childhood privy: 'When you took the lid off, you didn't know what was in the dark hole. To get in, you'd 'ave t' get round in this corner, shut the door, and then you were in the dark. Completely dark. Even in good sunlight it's dark in there.'

One's imagination didn't help either! Allison Randlesome talked of 'the ghostly hauntings that tapped at the wooden door, eerie shadows creeping under the door, the latch becoming stuck, as heart pounding, one tried to release it, the headless highwayman holding on tightly the other side, as the poor victim watched despairingly as the batteries in the torch expired!' And it was not just children who feared the worst. Chris Braddon of Fiddlers Green mentioned former occupants of their cottage who 'used to hold great get-togethers with neighbours and friends. Jack Andrew was a great storyteller and late at night he would turn the gas lamp down and tell the scariest ghost stories. Of course before some of the guests left for home they needed to visit the privy at the bottom of the garden, but I have been told they would prefer to walk home cross-legged unless absolutely desperate or visit in pairs as they had been spooked out by Jack's ghost stories.'

It was stinging nettles that made perhaps the biggest impression on Gloria Stephens, talking of the privy at Penhale Farm, Conce Moor that she knew when she was child. 'It was a tiny wooden shed like a sentry box, with a galvanised roof, and a little door that never really fitted. It just pulled to enough to give you the privacy you needed. It was just big enough to step in, turn around and sit down. It had a wooden seat with a bucket underneath, which was overflowing. I remember it mostly because it had the strongest, the biggest and the highest stinging nettles around it. As children we all tended to wear short little dresses and I got stung on the legs every time I went there. I dreaded going to this little toilet at the bottom of the garden. I remember it painfully well.'

Sinking into a cesspit must have been everyone's worst nightmare – but disaster-by-bog would have been most likely to occur on a farm. Derek Thomas told me of the occasion they took the cow to the bull on a nearby farm and thought things had gone swimmingly, until they saw the farmer's wife come rushing out, waving her arms about. She drew their attention to an important visitor, who had inadvertently strayed onto the cesspit, and was gradually sinking. 'These cesspits; they were open, and they were dreadful. As you walked across you could see where the grass was greenest, and that's where the cesspit would be. It just gently wobbled. Once you started sinking, you sank quite quickly, and the more you struggled, the worse it got, and the deeper you went. We managed to get him out, but his friends didn't want to know him for about a week after that!'

MULTI-OCCUPANCY!

Mavis Harris remembered, 'There was no lock on the privy door; just a latch. But you'd usually know where people were. If you heard footsteps coming down the garden, you'd yell, "'Ang on a minute. I'm in here!'" But this 'engaged' signal didn't work for the farmer's wife on the B & B farm that

Carrie Ham told me about. A modern cautionary tale! She thought she could function on automatic pilot after dark, as she knew where everything was. 'One night she wanted to go to the toilet, so she went as quietly as she could without putting any lights on, because she didn't want to interrupt anyone. So she got into the toilet, pulled up her nightie and went to sit down. But there was a man in there already, and she found herself sitting on his lap! She got out quick, and ran off! And the next day at breakfast time her husband said to her, "Oh, darling, we 'ad a visitor come in late last night. You'd gone to bed and I didn't tell you about it. Let me introduce you. . ." Then the man said, "No, that's quite all right. We've met already!"'

[9]

PRIVIES TODAY

Most people now have indoor sanitation and the little buildings at the end of the garden path may now serve as garden sheds, toolsheds, coalsheds, playhouses or animal shelters.

Privies are very much part of our heritage and the historical and architectural value of these charming old structures has become increasingly recognised in recent years. The Bagshawe family, for example, who now occupy the ancient moorland farmhouse at Codda in the parish of Altarnun, are very proud that their lovingly restored two-seater has achieved Grade II Listed status. Chloe told me, 'We got a grant from the Cornish Landscape Trust, who helped us rebuild the privy. It's particularly pretty, I think. We found a template of the seat, so my husband rebuilt it from that. So it's as original as we can get it.' The former builders of the privy skilfully harnessed a spring rising high on the hill and running through medieval drains, beneath a field and a wall into a trough, then through a gully and straight through the back of the privy, providing an ever constant flush.

Discovering a privy in the garden came as a pleasant surprise to Dutchman Steven Kaack and his wife, Carey, who run a market garden at Godolphin Cross. They always knew that a shed lurked beneath a heavy mantle of ivy, and were vaguely aware that there was more to the space thus enshrouded than met the eye. 'We found the old stone privy one day as we were digging out the flowerbed behind it, and

The privy at Godolphin Cross, which the Kaack family never knew they had.

as you can see, it is an earth closet – a bench with a hole in. Very basic. It was quite a find! I don't think we'll put it back in working order though, it's probably nicer to leave it ivy clad.' There is a lot to be said for a romantic ruin, and it seemed appropriate that such a discovery was made by someone who turned out to be a civil engineer, who had worked on state-of-the-art sewerage schemes in some of the world's most arid areas.

But perhaps the biggest pleasure for me in my Cornish privy search was to come across some serene pockets of privy contentment and to discover that the privy lives on!

My memorable meeting with Hilda Bennett and Leonard Masters in the hamlet of Penrose provided a rare and refreshing insight into life in rural Cornwall in days gone by – and right up to the present time. As far as I am concerned, my Champion of the Cornish Privy accolade should be jointly bestowed upon Leonard in Penrose and Arthur Richards of Bodmin Moor who have never known anything else. For having been born at St Columb early in the 20th century, Leonard has experienced life and earth closets on farms at Trevethan, Tregaswith, Bospolbans and Treburrick, before arriving here in 1942. He still makes use of the bucket-style traditional privy, depositing the content in the garden every day. In response to my question as to whether he would like to have modern indoor facilities, this delightful, gentle old man smiled and said, 'I dunno. I'm use ter what I've got, now. I'm gone 86; I shan't change now.'

The Reynolds family retained their privy at Buryas Bridge when mains water came, despite having a water closet indoors. This paid off when Lloyd broke his leg and was unable to get upstairs to use it. As far as Lloyd's children were concerned, the privy in the garden was part of their imaginative world, and daughter Stephanie remembered

Leonard Masters surveys the world from the security of his privy, which has served him well since the 1940s.

having camp fires in the garden, and using it as their kitchen. Lloyd recognises the importance of preserving the privy for future generations, as part of the heritage. 'Mustn't be let go, all these things. 'Cos once they're gone they're gone!'